DRIVE AND SURVIVL

DRIVE AND SURVIVE

A TEST-YOURSELF GUIDE

Gordon Cole

KOGAN
PAGE

First published in 1990 by
Kogan Page Ltd,
120 Pentonville Rd, London N1 9JN
in association with Castrol UK Ltd,
Burmah House, Pipers Way, Swindon SN3 1RE

Typeset by
DP Photosetting, Aylesbury, Bucks
Printed and bound in Great Britain by
Richard Clay Ltd, Bungay, Suffolk

British Library Cataloguing in Publication Data
Cole, Gordon
  Drive and survive.
  1. Motor vehicles.
  I. Title
  629.28'3

  ISBN 0–7494–0069–2

For the purposes of this book the majority of the photographs were composed in controlled circumstances. However, the author would like to point out that the photographs accompanying questions 153, 199, 200 and 201 are of real incidents, with which the author is in no way associated.

For further information about the Castrol Product Range please contact:

Consumer Relations Department,
Castrol (UK) Limited,
Burmah House,
Pipers Way,
Swindon,
Wiltshire SN3 1RE
Telephone (0793) 512712

For further information about the Castrol Product Range please contact:

Consumer Relations Department,
Castrol (UK) Limited,
Burmah House,
Pipers Way,
Swindon,
Wiltshire SN3 1RE
Telephone (0793) 512712

CONTENTS

FOREWORD

We all think that we use the highways and by-ways safely. In reality, unfortunately, this is not the case, judging by the alarming catalogue of road accidents which maim and kill every day in the UK.

Castrol is keen to promote the safer use of our roads and to contribute to the reduction of such accidents. We believe that achieving those objectives will be made easier by this new book. The clearly-illustrated on and off-road situations will prompt you to analyse your normal reactions, help you learn to anticipate danger and teach you to take the correct action when dealing with potentially hazardous incidents.

We hope that you will enjoy learning from this Castrol-sponsored publication and, more importantly, that it will allow you to *Drive and Survive*.

Dawn Adams
Castrol Educational Division

PREFACE

There are 36 million people in the United Kingdom who enjoy the privilege of holding a driving licence. A further three million people hold provisional driving licences. They represent numerous nationalities and are from all walks of life. Their attitude to life, and to other people's safety, can vary considerably. They all hold a licence to drive a motor vehicle. How they drive is another story, as accident statistics prove.

This book has been produced to help you avoid being involved in road accidents. There are over 200 pictures of real-life motoring situations within this book, with questions and multi-choice answers. Should you get some of the answers wrong, you are advised to consider seriously taking remedial action to improve your road craft, not only to preserve your own safety, but that of your family and other road users.

This can be achieved by attending one of the numerous driver improvement schemes that are available throughout the United Kingdom. Further details about these courses can be obtained by contacting your local Road Safety Officer at your Civic Centre or Town Hall. Information can also be acquired from the Institute of Advanced Motorists (01-994 4403) and RoSPA Advanced Drivers Association (021-233 2461), who will be pleased to assist you.

A test is not always a requirement on the conclusion of the course, but there is a lot to be gained, if you do decide to take one.

Gordon Cole
November 1989

ACKNOWLEDGEMENTS

I thank my friends most sincerely for the time and patience necessary to arrange the photographs.

Highways Economics Note Road Accident Costs 1987: supplied by the Department of Transport.

Developing and Printing by Kenton Photographic Colour Laboratories Ltd (01-206 0226).

All photographs taken by the author on Leica R6.

Drive & Survive UK Ltd are the owners of the registered trademark Drive & Survive. Drive & Survive offer a variety of advanced driving and skid control courses throughout the UK. These courses are available to both individuals and companies. For further details telephone 0245 466749 or fax 0245 460742, or write to Drive & Survive UK Ltd, Ford Motorsport, Boreham Airfield, Boreham, Chelmsford, Essex CM3 3BG.

The Highway Code is one of the most well-thumbed books in the country, but so often it is discarded the moment a person passes his or her driving test. In this excellent book, **Drive and Survive**, Gordon Cole has illustrated the rules of the road with over 200 questions and photographs of actual motoring situations. In so doing he provides an easy-to-read and fun way of revising the *Code* and testing yourself, whether you are an experienced or a novice driver, a motorcyclist, cyclist or pedestrian. As an experienced driver myself, in all kinds of road and weather conditions, I certainly have learned from it.

Ted Clements MBE
Chief Examiner
Institute of Advanced Motorists

INTRODUCTION

It can be said that once the driving test has been passed, the majority of drivers who do so forget, or ignore, the advice given in the Highway Code, and allow their standard of driving to deteriorate in many ways.

For example, they allow themselves to slip into habits which they think are better, easier, or just convenient. The first sign of deterioration is crossing the hands while turning the steering wheel. I have been told by some of those who do it, that 'it seems easier to turn, and anyway racing drivers do it, don't they?' Loss of steering control can, and often does occur, while crossing the hands.

There are drivers who cut right-hand corners while turning right: not of necessity because of the length of the vehicle (HGV), but because it is considered easier than following the correct line which gives maximum visibility and also allows for the sometimes rapid approach of other vehicles. What other road users should do when approaching the junction is not the prime concern of the lazy driver who takes a short cut while turning right!

Then there are those who rely on their so called 'right of way' whenever they use the roads. This dangerous attitude has in all probability originated in the fact that a next-to-worthless or a company-owned vehicle is being driven. This 'couldn't care less' frame of mind has the ingredients of an accident in the making.

Another serious and potentially dangerous driving fault committed every day, on all types of roads, at all speeds and in all weather conditions, is drivers deciding to change course without reasonable consideration for other road users. The use of the mirrors can be a bonus to someone else, but even when they are used, the information received is often ignored. The direction indicator signal may be considered an option, as is the effort required to use it, but often the option is not taken up. Then, regardless of what is passing, about to pass, or following, a change of course is made. Consequently, a serious or fatal accident can occur.

These four examples of bad driving indicate the attitude of many people who use our overcrowded roads every day. The dangerous faults they commit would not be tolerated during the driving test. It can be said that the attitude they have adopted can be the beginning of their end, as 5,000 people die in road accidents in the United Kingdom each year. Maybe they thought they knew all about driving or riding, but accident reports prove that a lot of them did not know all the answers.

The sad fact of life is that a lot of innocent people are killed because of another person's selfish or arrogant attitude while driving a motor vehicle. Accident reports have proved this fact time and time again. Accidents don't just happen: they are caused. It has been said that any fool can drive a motor vehicle – and a lot of them do.

To give an insight into what a road accident costs, the

information below should be borne in mind, especially when you feel your concentration is deteriorating, otherwise you could be included in the next set of statistics!

Total road accident costs in Great Britain in 1987

In 1987 4,694 fatal accidents, 54,352 serious accidents and 180,014 slight accidents were reported. The cost of these 239,060 accidents is estimated to have been £3,991 million at 1987 prices. In addition, there were an estimated 1,423,000 damage-only accidents costing a further £995 million. Thus, total accident costs in 1987 were estimated to have been £4,985 million.

These figures give serious and slight casualty costs calculated, as in previous years, from the following items:

Loss of output due to injury. This is calculated as the present value of the expected loss of earnings plus any non-wage payments (national insurance contributions, etc) paid by the employer.

Ambulance costs and the costs of hospital treatment.

The cost of pain, grief and suffering to the casualty, relatives and friends that can never be truly calculated.

Although they are considered important, the evaluation of these costs presents difficulties; consequently, a notional sum has been included in the estimated cost of serious and slight casualties.

It is clear that road accidents are expensive, not only in financial terms, but in pain, suffering and hardship. The majority of accidents that occur could have been prevented. *Accidents do not just happen, they are caused.*

The majority of people who hold a driving licence think they are good drivers. *How* good are you? Study each picture and compare the answers under each. Mark your answer on a separate piece of paper, then check your answers against those at the end of the book.

Other books by Gordon Cole, who has worked in driver training for over thirty years, include: *Advanced Driving, Pass The Driving Test, Take Your Car Abroad.*

DRIVING PLAN

1

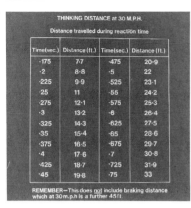

THINKING DISTANCE at 30 M.P.H.

Distance travelled during reaction time

Time(sec.)	Distance (ft.)	Time(sec.)	Distance (ft.)
·175	7·7	·475	20·9
·2	8·8	·5	22
·225	9·9	·525	23·1
·25	11	·55	24·2
·275	12·1	·575	25·3
·3	13·2	·6	26·4
·325	14·3	·625	27·5
·35	15·4	·65	28·6
·375	16·5	·675	29·7
·4	17·6	·7	30·8
·425	18·7	·725	31·9
·45	19·8	·75	33

REMEMBER—This does <u>not</u> include braking distance which at 30 m.p.h is a further 45 ft

1. The average driver takes 0.7 seconds from seeing an emergency situation to placing a foot on the brake pedal. This can be defined as the reaction time. If travelling at 30 mph on a good, dry road what is the overall stopping distance at this speed?

(A) 40 feet.
(B) 55 feet.
(C) 75 feet.

2. You are following another vehicle on a dual-carriageway that has a national speed limit of 70 mph. Both vehicles are travelling at 60 mph, the road surface is dry. The distance between the two vehicles is 216 feet. Should the vehicle in front suddenly stop due to mechanical failure, have you allowed an adequate margin of safety to be able to stop before colliding with the vehicle in front? The shortest overall stopping distance at 60 mph is:

(A) 240 feet?
(B) 216 feet?
(C) 315 feet?

3. If this vehicle was travelling at 70 mph how many feet per second would the vehicle cover?

(A) 30 feet.
(B) 103 feet.
(C) 88 feet.

4. There are some drivers who are not aware of the road and weather conditions. What do you think was the prime factor that caused this accident?

(A) The weather.
(B) Speed.
(C) The lamppost.

5. How frequently should a driver use the mirror or mirrors, thus being aware of what is following?

(A) Every few seconds.
(B) Before changing course.
(C) Now and again.

7. As you arrive at a 'T' junction, you glance quickly to either side and decide to emerge. Is it safe to do so?

(A) It looks clear.
(B) Yes.
(C) No.

6. Medicines have been collected from a doctor's surgery. What must be checked before taking the medicines and driving a motor vehicle?

(A) The quantity of the medicine is correct.
(B) The medicines are the correct treatment for the ailment suffered.
(C) Consumption of the medicine will not have any adverse influence on the ability to drive a motor vehicle.

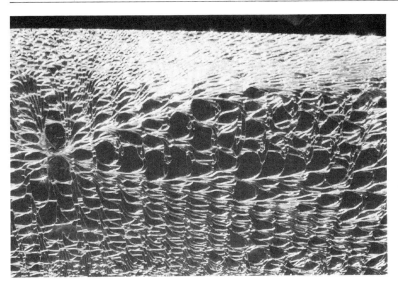

8. This is a driver's view of a toughened windscreen at the moment it shatters. What should you do if this should happen while driving at 50 mph?

(A) Brake hard and stop.
(B) Punch a hole in the screen.
(C) Make effective use of your mirror, slow down and signal your intention to pull into the side of the road.

9. The driver approached this left-hand bend too fast and has lost control of the vehicle. The rear of the car is sliding to the offside and the driver has turned the steering wheel to the right. Is this correct?

(A) Yes.
(B) No.
(C) He should have centralised.

10. Should a driver of a Heavy Goods Vehicle with a gross weight of 17.5 T approach this bridge, what action, if any, should the driver take?

(A) The driver proceeds over the bridge as the road ahead seems to be clear.
(B) The driver thinks he is within the law and therefore proceeds over the bridge.
(C) The driver checks the mirrors then signals to stop. The vehicle should be turned around and another route found.

11. A warning sign can be seen and so can an articulated vehicle which is using the whole width of the road due to its length. What course of action should you take in this situation?

(A) Continue at the same speed.
(B) Make effective use of the mirrors and reduce speed.
(C) Sound the horn and expect the lorry to pass you by the time you reach the bend.

12. Stubble is being burnt in the field. What danger can arise as you pass it?

(A) The heat from the fire could make you drowsy.
(B) The smoke could make you cough.
(C) The smoke could be swirling and in doing so blow across the road, reducing visibility drastically.

13. Should speed be reduced on the approach to a hump bridge?

(A) Yes.
(B) No.
(C) Not sure.

14. The driver on the right has made a decision to overtake. Is it a safe place to start an overtaking manoeuvre?

(A) Yes.
(B) The road is wide enough.
(C) No.

15. What colour are the lights to which the traffic sign refers?

(A) Amber.
(B) Red.
(C) Green.

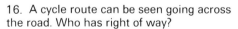

16. A cycle route can be seen going across the road. Who has right of way?

(A) Drivers and riders on the road.
(B) Cyclists on the cycle route.
(C) Neither.

17. While driving in slow moving traffic, your intention is to turn left at the next junction. Using your mirrors, you see a cyclist moving fast on your near side. What should you do?

(A) Continue as you intended before the mirrors were used.
(B) Stop and let the cyclist pass, then check the mirrors again before turning left.
(C) Sound the horn and turn, and force the cyclist to stop.

18. In fog rear fog lamps should be used when visibility is seriously reduced; especially when you cannot see more than a certain distance. What is that distance?

(A) 50 metres.
(B) 75 metres.
(C) 100 metres.

19. Is the driver overtaking at a safe place?

(A) Yes.
(B) Not sure.
(C) No.

20. This driver is obsessed by speed and has not planned far enough ahead. On seeing the deep surface water, what course of action should have been adopted to prevent the potentially dangerous situation arising?

(A) The horn should be used to warn other drivers of his presence.
(B) The mirrors should be used and speed reduced by 5 mph.
(C) The mirrors should be used, speed reduced and, if safe to do so, a change in course made to near the centre of the road.

21. This vehicle is moving slowly, sucking up the surplus stone chippings off the road. The view to the left-hand side of the vehicle is obscured by the presence of the lorry. Should the decision to overtake be made?

(A) Yes.
(B) No.
(C) Not sure.

22. The police have arrived at the scene of an accident in which a motorcyclist, on leaving a roundabout, has collided with a car coming in the opposite direction. If the rider and driver had taken an advanced riding/driving course, should the accident have occurred?

(A) Most probably not.
(B) Yes.
(C) Not sure.

24. The driver has reduced speed to allow a pedestrian to cross the crossing. The driver has decided to move off. Has an offence been committed? If so, by whom?

(A) The pedestrian.
(B) Neither.
(C) The driver.

23. When there is a continuous white line in the centre of the road as shown, you must not cross or straddle it except in certain circumstances. How many circumstances are there listed in the *Highway Code*?

(A) Two.
(B) Five.
(C) Four.

26. The driver is lighting a cigarette while driving. What danger can arise while doing so?

(A) None.
(B) The lighter could fail to work.
(C) The driver could lose control of the vehicle.

25. A car is being driven over an area of diagonal stripes while overtaking another vehicle. What advice is given in the *Highway Code* regarding the action taken by the driver who is overtaking?

(A) It is permitted to drive over an area of diagonal stripes while overtaking.
(B) It is possible to drive over an area of diagonal stripes providing the full length of the area is not covered.
(C) You should not overtake where it would involve driving over an area marked with diagonal stripes or chevrons if you can avoid doing so.

27. This single-carriageway (undivided) road has three lanes. Who has priority to use the middle lane?

(A) Traffic travelling down the hill.
(B) No one, regardless what direction they are travelling.
(C) Traffic travelling up hill.

28. A driver is stopping at a junction to take effective observation. At the same time another driver has decided to overtake. Is the action being taken by the overtaking driver complying with the *Highway Code*?

(A) No.
(B) Yes, providing it is safe to do so.
(C) Yes.

29. A vehicle can be seen overtaking. Another vehicle has just joined the road and in doing so has blocked the path of the overtaking vehicle. In this situation one of the drivers must take evasive action to prevent an accident. Which one?

(A) The driver on the left should accelerate.
(B) The driver on the right should look in the mirrors, reduce speed, and return to the left-hand side of the road.
(C) The driver ahead should reverse to where he emerged from.

30. The view of the pedestrian crossing is obscured by works vehicles. Therefore, how should the driver approach the pedestrian crossing?

(A) The driver should make effective use of the mirrors, reduce speed and be able to stop should the situation demand it.
(B) The driver should sound the horn and maintain the present speed.
(C) No pedestrians can be seen, therefore the driver can signal to move out to pass the obstruction and proceed as normal.

31. A vehicle is approaching a zebra crossing. A pedestrian has stepped on to the crossing. Who has right of way?

(A) The driver.
(B) Neither.
(C) The pedestrian.

32. While on a journey a violent thunderstorm occurs. Hailstones can be seen bouncing off the road. What would you do in this situation?

(A) Reduce speed, switch the headlights on with the beam dipped.
(B) Continue at your normal speed because you think the tyres can cope with the excess water on the road.
(C) Your journey has to be completed within a given time so you do not consider reducing speed.

33. From what can be seen who has priority: the pedestrian, the driver on the left or the driver on the right?

(A) The pedestrian.
(B) The approaching driver.
(C) The driver on the left.

34. The time is 3.30 pm on a week day. With the information that can be seen, why is the driver reducing speed?

(A) Because it is a pretty village.
(B) Because the driving is going to stop at the Inn for a meal.
(C) Because school children could be leaving school.

35. The driver on the left has reduced speed in the interest of the safety of the pedestrian, who can be seen approaching. The action taken by the driver was done because another vehicle was overtaking at the time. Which of the drivers is at fault?

(A) The driver on the left.
(B) The driver on the right.
(C) Both.

36. This driver is seen driving with one hand on the roof. What advantage is gained by this action?

(A) Car control is improved.
(B) It makes a contribution to road safety.
(C) No advantage.

37. The young cyclist is riding too close to the road. Is the driver taking the correct action by reducing speed?

(A) No.
(B) Yes.
(C) No sure.

38. You have just got into your vehicle and are about to move off. You look in the mirrors and see a vehicle, about 100 yards behind, approaching you. What would you do?

(A) Wait until the vehicle passes, then move off if safe to do so.
(B) Signal your intention to move out, then do so.
(C) Release the handbrake then accelerate quickly before the approaching vehicle reaches you.

39. As you approach a left-hand bend you can see numerous pot-holes ahead, most of which are filled with water. You can see how wide they are but not how deep. How should you approach the bend?

(A) Look well ahead, use the mirrors, then, if safe to do so, go round the pot-holes.
(B) Drive on, regardless of the road surface. Your vehicle has excellent suspension, therefore you will not feel any discomfort.
(C) If another road user is following, stop and wave him on. Then estimate the depth of the hole, determining how big the splash will be if you continue driving on the same course.

40. Ahead of you can be seen a slow moving vehicle that will hinder your progress. You have therefore made the decision to overtake, but before doing so would you:

(A) Wait until the vehicle in front has passed the stationary vehicles and a full and constant view of the road ahead can be seen?
(B) Drive close to the rear of the vehicle in front and give a long horn note, to warn the driver in front to move over and give you more of the road to carry out your manoeuvre?
(C) Think the road ahead is clear, and overtake on the basis of information that can and cannot be seen?

41. As you approach a line of parked vehicles, you can see the road ahead is clear and the decision is made to pass them. As you pass the first vehicle, another road user has come round a bend and is in your path. In this situation would you:

(A) Apply the brakes and stop where you are?
(B) Drive on and force the approaching driver to stop and, if possible, let you pass?
(C) Use the mirrors and pull into the gap on the left, allowing the approaching driver right of way in doing so?

42. While driving in snow and slush, what would be the most suitable gear to select to obtain maximum traction? You are trying to maintain a road speed of 15 mph. Would it be:

(A) First gear?
(B) Second gear?
(C) Third gear?

43. As you approach this humpback bridge, you notice that the mirrors have been vandalised. What procedure should you adopt?

(A) None, continue driving at the present speed of 20 mph.
(B) Select a lower gear to be able to accelerate up the hill more quickly.
(C) Look in your mirrors, reduce speed, select a lower gear then sound the horn to inform others of your presence.

44. The uncompleted road surface and protruding manhole covers can cause expensive damage to a vehicle. How should this road be negotiated to reduce the risk of damage?

(A) Drive over the centre of the manhole covers.
(B) Stop before each manhole cover, then drive slowly over it in a high gear.
(C) Without causing any inconvenience to any other road user, the course should be altered slightly to avoid the tyres making contact with the manhole covers.

45. As you approach this narrow archway pedestrians can be seen on the road. Should you:

(A) Look in the mirrors, reduce speed and/or stop until the road ahead is clear of pedestrians, then proceed?
(B) Sound the horn and expect the pedestrians to move out of your way?
(C) Continue driving at the same speed, then brake hard as you near the pedestrians?

46. As you approach this narrow bridge a vehicle can be seen approaching; both of you are the same distance from the arch. No information or warning signs are present to indicate who has priority. What should you do?

(A) Look in the mirrors, reduce speed and prepare to stop. Then let the driver of the approaching vehicle dictate the situation, bearing in mind that neither of you has the right of way.
(B) Sound the horn, flash the headlights and maintain your present speed of 20 mph.
(C) Accelerate hard hoping to get through the arch first.

47. No warning signs have been displayed to inform road users that white lining is in progress, as can be seen by the position of the works lorry. On the approach to this situation, bearing in mind what can and cannot be seen, would you:

(A) Pass the works lorry on the left?
(B) Sound the horn and continue to drive past the lorry on the left?
(C) Look in the mirrors and stop. Then proceed when you are sure it is safe to do so, at the same time sounding the horn to warn the workman of your presence, while steering to the right of the lorry?

48. As you approach road works on your side of the road, a bus can be seen approaching you. Would you:

(A) Signal your intention to move out into a position to pass the road works?
(B) Flash the headlights to warn the bus driver of your presence, at the same time changing course to pass the road works?
(C) Look in the mirrors, reduce speed and wait for the bus to pass?

49. This driver has stopped to take some refreshment – beer with a high alcohol content. What advice does the *Highway Code* give regarding drinking and driving?

(A) It is permitted provided the blood alcohol level does not exceed 82mg/105ml.
(B) You must not drive under the influence of drink.
(C) You may drink and drive provided you do not exceed your limit.

50. The driver is turning left, at the same time as a pedestrian is crossing the road. Who has the right of way?

(A) The pedestrian.
(B) The driver.
(C) Neither.

51. The driver is stopping at a zebra crossing to let a pedestrian cross the road. Why is the driver giving an arm signal to slow down?

(A) To inform other road users and pedestrians of the intention to slow down or stop at the zebra crossing.
(B) It is the ideal place to practice an arm signal.
(C) To encourage the pedestrian to hurry.

52. This driver has stopped at a zebra crossing and is giving a signal to the pedestrian, inviting him to cross the road. Is this the correct thing to do?

(A) Yes, if it will assist the pedestrian.
(B) No, as you could put the safety of the pedestrian in danger.
(C) On occasions.

53. There is not enough room for these two vehicles to pass each other safely, therefore they have stopped. The approaching driver is flashing his headlights. What advice is given in the *Highway Code* regarding flashing headlamps?

(A) It is an invitation for you to proceed.
(B) It lets another road user know you are there.
(C) It lets you know the driver is in a hurry.

54. A driver is seen turning left at a 'T' junction while looking right. The presence of the vehicle approaching from the left has not been noted, because effective observation has not been made before the driver started to emerge. If you were the driver of the approaching car, what would you do in this situation?

(A) Continue at the present speed and course.
(B) Sound the horn.
(C) Look in the mirrors, sound the horn, reduce speed and prepare to stop.

56. This driver is going to pass a row of stationary vehicles. Has enough room been allowed to pass with an adequate margin of safety?

(A) Yes.
(B) No.
(C) Could be.

55. This driver is waiting to turn right. A vehicle can be seen approaching, indicating his intention to turn left by means of a direction indicator signal. If you were the driver on the right, would you start to emerge on the basis of what can be seen?

(A) Yes.
(B) No.
(C) Not sure.

57. A vehicle can be seen emerging from private property, at the same time as a pedestrian is seen using the pavement. Who has the right of way?

(A) Neither.
(B) The driver.
(C) The pedestrian.

MOTORWAYS

2

58. Motorists about to join the motorway are warned that the road surface is slippery, more so when wet. With this information in mind how would you approach the slip road?

(A) Select a lower gear and accelerate.
(B) Look in the mirrors and relax the pressure on the accelerator until the curve has been passed. Then gently accelerate when on the straight, if safe to do so.
(C) Continue at the same speed as you would normally.

59. Warning signals can be seen at the start of a slip road leading to the motorway. Should amber lights start to flash and no message be shown, the information given warns drivers that they should not exceed a certain speed. What is that speed?

(A) 50 mph.
(B) 60 mph.
(C) 30 mph.

60. This driver is reversing along a slip road on a motorway because it was joined by mistake. Is the action being taken by the driver within the law?

(A) Yes.
(B) Sometimes.
(C) No.

61. Vehicles are about to join a motorway by a slip lane then by an acceleration lane. Who has right of way – vehicles on the motorway or vehicles about to join the motorway?

(A) Vehicles about to join the motorway.
(B) Neither.
(C) Vehicles on the motorway.

62. As you proceed along this slip road to join the motorway, a traffic sign can be seen. What information do you gather from the sign?

(A) The acceleration lane becomes the nearside lane, therefore the number of lanes is increased.
(B) There is an extended acceleration lane ahead.
(C) The hard shoulder should be used, until directed otherwise.

63. A pedestrian can be seen running along the hard shoulder of a motorway carrying a petrol can. Another road user has stopped to give the pedestrian a lift. How many offences, if any, are being committed?

(A) One.
(B) Two.
(C) Three.

64. At about 110-metre intervals white marker posts are placed on the verge of the hard shoulder on a motorway. What information do the posts give a driver?

(A) It is a countdown marker to the next exit.
(B) It shows the direction to the nearest public telephone.
(C) It informs a driver of the direction to the nearest emergency telephone.

65. On motorways the emergency phone boxes are placed at intervals of 1½ km on both sides of the motorway, and are sited on the verge at the back of the hard shoulder. They are orange in colour, and are identified by a number, letter and 'SOS'. Should an emergency or a vehicle breakdown occur and assistance is required, the emergency phone will have to be used. No money is required to do so. When the phone is used who will answer?

(A) The police.
(B) A motoring organisation.
(C) The Highways Department of the county you are in.

66. This traffic sign can be seen on some motorways. What information does it give you?

(A) Vehicles two metres and over should use the outside lane.
(B) The two open lanes are being diverted to the left, therefore the hard shoulder should be used for vehicles two metres and over.
(C) All traffic in the nearside lane will be diverted off the motorway 800 yards ahead. Vehicles two metres wide and over have the option of continuing on the motorway.

67. The temporary traffic sign can be seen on the approach to road works on motorways. The message it gives is precise. What other information should a driver of a vehicle 2.9 metres wide or over expect to see further along the carriageway?

(A) All drivers of vehicles 2.9 metres and over stop here and contact the police.
(B) The nearside lane must be used. Maximum speed 20 mph.
(C) The outside lane must be used. Proceed with caution.

68. On this motorway the information given by the signs on the gantry over the road can be clearly seen. If you are in doubt whether to leave the motorway at the next exit, what should you do?

(A) Steer on to the hard shoulder and stop, then check on a map to see where you are.
(B) Stop at the next emergency telephone and seek advice as to your whereabouts.
(C) Take the next exit off the motorway. Once off the motorway stop where it is legal and safe to do so, then check your position on the map.

69. The Heavy Goods Vehicles are travelling at 50 mph on a motorway. Are the drivers observing the 'two-second rule', ie the minimum stopping distance?

(A) Yes.
(B) No.
(C) Not sure.

70. The nearside lane is clear of traffic, but the driver of this car has decided the middle lane is more suitable than the nearside lane. What potentially dangerous situation could occur because of the selfish action taken by this driver?

(A) Vehicles travelling faster on the nearside lane can overtake on the left.
(B) No danger will arise provided a steady 55 mph is maintained.
(C) Heavy Goods Vehicles cannot use the outside lane, or overtake on the nearside lane. Therefore this inconsiderate driver will block their path.

71. On the M1 one of the vehicles in this picture is breaking the law. Which one is it?

(A) The vehicle in the nearside lane.
(B) The vehicle in the middle lane.
(C) The vehicle in the outside lane.

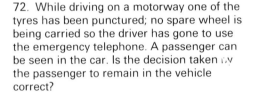

72. While driving on a motorway one of the tyres has been punctured; no spare wheel is being carried so the driver has gone to use the emergency telephone. A passenger can be seen in the car. Is the decision taken by the passenger to remain in the vehicle correct?

(A) Yes, it is the safest place to be.
(B) No, the passenger should leave the vehicle from the nearside and take refuge on the high banked area of grass while the driver is away.
(C) The passenger should assist the driver by getting the jack out of the boot, and in doing so assist the breakdown service when it arrives.

73. There is traffic congestion on this motorway. A driver can be seen using the hard shoulder to jump the queue of traffic to get to the service centre. Is the action taken by the driver on the hard shoulder within the law?

(A) No.
(B) Yes.
(C) Probably.

74. The driver of this vehicle did not check the amount of fuel available in the tank before joining the motorway, and has run out of fuel. Consequently he has stopped on the hard shoulder. Has the vehicle been stopped in the correct place on the hard shoulder?

(A) Yes, it is safe on the hard shoulder.
(B) The vehicle could be parked nearer the white line.
(C) No. The vehicle should be parked as far to the left as possible.

75. Do you think the driver who is towing the caravan is complying with the 'two-second rule'?

(A) Yes.
(B) Not sure.
(C) No.

76. An accident has occurred on a motorway, other drivers have stopped to assist if possible. How many new dangers have been created by people not involved in the accident?

(A) One.
(B) Three.
(C) Four.

77. While driving along a motorway the sign on the left may be seen. What information does the sign give you.

(A) Traffic joining the motorway will do so in an additional lane, therefore there will be three lanes half a mile ahead.
(B) Traffic in the nearside lane should turn off at the next exit which is half a mile ahead.
(C) The hard shoulder should be used half a mile ahead.

78. Owing to road works being carried out, the speed limit on this motorway is 50 mph. How many obvious driving faults can you see being committed?

(A) None.
(B) One.
(C) Two.

79. While driving along a motorway during a thunderstorm your view of the road ahead is obscured by the volume of spray being thrown up by the Heavy Goods Vehicle. How can you improve your view of the road ahead?

(A) Switch the headlamps on to main beam.
(B) Change course to the lane on your right.
(C) Look in the mirrors and, if safe to do so, reduce speed gradually.

80. This traffic sign on a motorway gives adequate and clear information. At what distance from an exit is the first advance information sign placed which informs drivers there is an exit ahead?

(A) 1 mile.
(B) 2 miles.
(C) ½ mile.

81. While travelling on a three-lane motorway you see this sign. What information do you glean from it?

(A) Traffic in the nearside lane must use the hard shoulder.
(B) The nearside lane is designated for traffic leaving the motorway at the next exit, therefore the number of lanes is reduced.
(C) There is a diversion in the nearside lane, therefore speed should be reduced.

82. Some slip roads leading off motorways and on the approach to roundabouts have yellow speed hatch markings to assist drivers. For what purpose have the hatch markings been provided?

(A) To inform drivers they are going too fast.
(B) To inform drivers they are on a slip lane.
(C) 'Count down' lines from the hazard.

RURAL ROADS

3

83. Ahead of you, long graduated bends can be seen. Where should you look to gain as much advance information as possible?

(A) Three hundred metres ahead.
(B) As far ahead as possible.
(C) The next bend.

84. As you enter a right-hand bend a vehicle can be seen leaving a driveway on the left. You have seen the car but the other driver has not seen you. In this situation would you:

(A) Continue to drive on the same course?
(B) Sound the horn and think to yourself the other driver can hear your warning of approach?
(C) Look in the mirrors, change course to the crown of the road and reduce speed?

85. On the approach to a left-hand bend on a country road, little or no advance observation of the road ahead is possible, due to the height of the hedge. How can you assess the severity of the bend?

(A) By looking at the top of the hedgerows.
(B) By the sudden appearance of approaching traffic.
(C) By noting where the offside and nearside verges appear to meet.

86. Wearing sunglasses and driving along a country road in bright sunshine, you are about to go through woodlands with a dark shaded area ahead of you. As you enter the heavy shadows, what can you do to assist your eyes to adapt to the sudden change of light?

(A) Switch on the headlights.
(B) Remove sunglasses.
(C) Use the windscreen wipers.

87. You approach a junction during a thunderstorm. Globules of water on the windows obscure the view to either side of you. What course of action would you take?

(A) Take what visibility there is for granted, and proceed when you think the road is clear.
(B) Open the side windows to gain a clear view of the road to either side of you.
(C) Wait for the rain to stop, then proceed.

88. A coal merchant's lorry has been stopped on the approach to a bend and the coalman can be seen beside the vehicle. What action would you take?

(A) Use the mirrors, reduce speed and anticipate having to stop.
(B) As you do not know what the coalman is going to do, you would sound the horn and pass him.
(C) Expect the driver of the approaching vehicle to stop and have a chat with the coalman, in which case you would sound the horn and demand right of way.

89. Three temporary traffic signs have been placed on the left-hand verge. The message given by two signs is obscured by undergrowth. In this situation would you:

(A) Continue driving at your normal speed and see what transpires?
(B) Look in the mirrors and if necessary reduce speed, so that you can stop within the distance you can see to be clear.
(C) Approach the signs with caution and stop beside each one, to identify the message given.

90. While driving in a rural area, you approach a junction and intend to turn left. The road surface is dry apart from a large puddle in front of you. What should you do?

(A) Ignore the puddle and drive through it.
(B) When you are sure it is safe to do so, go round the water because you do not know how deep it is.
(C) Turn right and in doing so bypass the water which you think is contaminated, because of its colour.

91. While driving along a country lane you see a tractor emerging from a field. What course of action would you take in this situation?

(A) Give a long horn note, and expect the tractor to reverse back into the field.
(B) Drive towards the nearside of the tractor, hoping that the driver sees you.
(C) Be patient and follow the tractor from a safe distance.

URBAN ROADS

92. A pedestrian can be seen standing next to a parked car, she could be locking or opening the door. What would you do in this situation?

(A) The mirrors should be used and a change of course made.
(B) No change of course or action is required.
(C) You consider your road position is ideal.

93. This driver is passing a row of stationary vehicles. Is an adequate margin of safety being allowed?

(A) No.
(B) Yes.
(C) Not sure.

94. A driver can be seen overtaking another vehicle within the area marked by zigzag lines. A pedestrian is on the zebra crossing. Is an offence being committed and if so, by whom?

A) The pedestrian.
B) The overtaking driver.
C) The driver who is stopping at the crossing.

95. Due to a long dry spell, the road surface has become very smooth. After a shower of rain, would rubber, dust and oil deposits have an adverse effect on vehicle control?

(A) Yes.
(B) No.
(C) Perhaps.

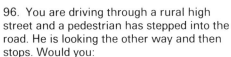

96. You are driving through a rural high street and a pedestrian has stepped into the road. He is looking the other way and then stops. Would you:

(A) Continue on your present course and expect the pedestrian to become aware of your presence?
(B) Wait until you get closer to the pedestrian, then sound the horn?
(C) Use the mirrors, sound the horn and anticipate having to stop, at the same time reducing speed?

97. As you approach a roundabout, your view to the right is obscured by parked vehicles. How should you approach the roundabout?

(A) Continue driving at the same speed until you can see what is approaching, then brake hard.
(B) Continue at the same speed and sound the horn to let other road users know you are there.
(C) Look in the mirrors and reduce speed so that you can stop smoothly, should the need arise.

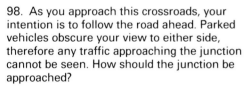

98. As you approach this crossroads, your intention is to follow the road ahead. Parked vehicles obscure your view to either side, therefore any traffic approaching the junction cannot be seen. How should the junction be approached?

(A) Maintain the present speed as you have the right of way.
(B) Sound the horn and continue without looking.
(C) The mirrors must be used then speed reduced, the horn is considered while looking right, left and right again.

99. While following this vehicle in slow moving traffic your view of the road ahead is restricted. What action could be taken to improve your view of the road ahead?

(A) Move towards the kerb.
(B) Move towards the centre of the road.
(C) Drop back from the vehicle.

SINGLE-TRACK ROADS

5

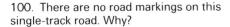

100. There are no road markings on this single-track road. Why?

(A) The road is not wide enough.
(B) There is no need for them.
(C) It is a class 'C' road.

101. You are driving along this lane, and a vehicle may be about to leave the second drive on the left. How would you know?

(A) The front of the vehicle will be seen as it comes into view.
(B) You will be able to hear the sound of the engine.
(C) You will see the shadow of the vehicle approaching the road.

102. As you approach this right-hand bend on a single-track road, a car, with its stop lights on, can be seen in a passing place. What should you anticipate from the information available?

(A) A vehicle could be approaching.
(B) The driver could be lost, and be looking at a map.
(C) The driver has stopped to look at the countryside.

103. While driving down a single-track road you can see a vehicle approaching. What should you do in this situation?

(A) Flash the headlights, and in doing so, expect the approaching driver to reduce speed and move over to his left to let you pass.
(B) Maintain the same speed and see what occurs.
(C) Look in the mirrors, reduce speed and stop in the gap on the left, making sure it is safe to do so.

104. While driving along a single-track road an oncoming vehicle can be seen. What should you do?

(A) Expect the approaching vehicle to reverse into a passing place that has been passed.
(B) A passing place is on your side of the road, therefore you should pull into it.
(C) You will have to reverse into a passing place that you have already passed on the offside of the road.

105. While driving along this single-track road two vehicles can be seen approaching you. Should you?

(A) Flash the headlights and expect the approaching vehicles to stop and reverse out of your way.
(B) Sound the horn and make an arm movement suggesting they should reverse.
(C) Look in the mirrors and stop. As there is no passing place at this section of road, there is no option but for you to reverse.

106. While driving along this single-track road, the driver has pulled into a passing place. Why do you think this recommended action was taken?

(A) It seems an ideal place to stop.
(B) To allow the driver behind to overtake.
(C) The driver has decided to stop and have a rest.

FLOODED ROADS

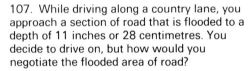

107. While driving along a country lane, you approach a section of road that is flooded to a depth of 11 inches or 28 centimetres. You decide to drive on, but how would you negotiate the flooded area of road?

(A) Drive on as if the water was not present, at the same time sounding the horn, just in case another road user should appear.

(B) Accelerate in the highest possible gear to obtain maximum traction.

(C) Move off slowly in first gear with the engine running fast, controlling the speed of the vehicle by use of the clutch.

108. You have stopped at the edge of a flooded road. Ahead of you a pedestrian can be seen trying to pass the water without getting his feet wet. Would you?

(A) Drive alongside the pedestrian and ask if he would like a lift, bearing in mind that the water by the pedestrian could be deep.

(B) Drive forward, at the same time sound the horn to warn the pedestrian of your presence.

(C) Wait at the water's edge until the pedestrian has passed the flooded area, then proceed.

109. The tractor drive has created a potentially dangerous situation to another road user, who is leaving a flooded area of the road. What action should have been taken by the tractor driver to avoid blocking the road?

(A) The tractor driver should have driven up the left-hand bank to let the approaching driver pass.
(B) He should have reversed, allowing the approaching driver to leave the flood water.
(C) The tractor driver should have looked across the bend, and having seen the approaching vehicle, should therefore have waited until it had passed.

110. A flood warning sign has been placed at the edge of the flooded road. Do you think the sign has been placed at the correct distance from the hazard?

(A) Yes.
(B) The sign should have been placed at least five metres from the edge of the flood water.
(C) The sign should have been placed further away from the hazard, so that road users have time to act on the information given.

111. As you arrive at the edge of a section of road that is flooded, a cyclist has started to negotiate the water. In this situation would you:

(A) Wait at the edge of the water until the cyclist has passed through the flooded area, then proceed?
(B) Proceed and overtake the cyclist?
(C) Sound the horn and drive on as though there were no water present?

112. This sign has been placed at the edge of the road – why? Is it because:

(A) The local authority is very road safety conscious?
(B) It's about time you did?
(C) You have just gone through flood water?

TRAFFIC
SIGNS

113. You may have seen this sign situated on the pavement next to the kerb. What is the purpose of the sign?

(A) It is requesting assistance to be given to another road user.
(B) The police are requesting information regarding a fatal road accident that has occurred.
(C) To encourage you to contact the local police station, for the purpose of helping them with their next fete.

114. The message given by the sign is clear. If police presence is not obvious should the warning sign be ignored?

(A) Yes.
(B) No.
(C) The sign is just there for effect.

115. The driver did not see the maximum speed limit sign when passing, and is not aware of the speed limit in this road. The lampposts are within 200 yards of each other, no repeater signs can be seen. What is the maximum speed a vehicle can travel within the law?

(A) 40 mph.
(B) 30 mph.
(C) 50 mph.

116. The traffic sign can be clearly seen. What should you anticipate happening 250 yards ahead?

(A) Nothing, as the road ahead can be seen to be clear.
(B) There is a side road on the left, a strong side wind could be present causing turbulence.
(C) Traffic could be emerging from the road on the left, therefore the mirrors should be used and speed reduced.

118. You are about to descend a steep hill and a warning sign can be seen advising you to try your brakes. Why?

(A) It is about time you did.
(B) As a safety precaution, to make sure that the brakes do work.
(C) It doesn't matter why, you should comply with the sign.

117. Two parents have parked their vehicles outside a school. How many hazards have been created?

(A) Three.
(B) Four.
(C) One.

119. While driving along a dual carriageway, you notice that hatch markings and red cylinders (posts) have been used. Why?

(A) To keep traffic away from the central reservation.

(B) To prevent traffic turning right at the next gap in the central reservation.

(C) To taper the road into a single lane, and in doing so, to prevent overtaking. Also to protect traffic turning right.

120. Road works are in progress on one side of a dual carriageway. To assist traffic flow one lane has been transferred to the other carriageway. What is this traffic flow system called?

(A) Contra-flow.

(B) Two-way traffic.

(C) Pass either side traffic.

121. A strong side wind can have an adverse effect on the cyclist, motorcyclist or driver. Is this because it:

(A) Interferes with the speed of the vehicle?
(B) Blows dust across the road?
(C) Interferes with steering ability?

122. You are approaching a junction that has a STOP sign. The other roads can be seen to be clear of traffic. Do you have to stop?

(A) No.
(B) You should almost stop.
(C) Yes.

123. You are approaching double mini-roundabouts with the intention of following the road ahead. Who has the right of way at the roundabouts?

A) Traffic approaching from the left.
B) Traffic approaching from the right.
C) Nobody.

124. A temporary traffic sign can be seen warning road users that the light signals controlling traffic are not working. Who has the right of way at the crossroads?

(A) Traffic approaching from the right.
(B) No one.
(C) Oncoming traffic.

125. The road surface has been re-laid and a recommended speed limit sign can be seen. What is the potential danger, should the recommendation be ignored?

(A) The paintwork on the vehicle could be damaged.
(B) It is illegal to exceed 20 mph.
(C) The loose chippings will have an adverse effect on the stopping distance and control of the vehicle.

126. The information on the traffic sign can be clearly seen. What do you think is the time of day, based on other information in the photograph?

(A) 7.30 am.
(B) 9.45 am.
(C) 3.30 pm.

127. The warning sign informs road users that there is a blind summit ahead. What other wording could have been used on this sign to convey the same meaning, and what is the danger?

(A) 'Steep Hill'. The road has a hump at the top.
(B) 'Dead Ground'. The road ahead cannot be seen to be clear.
(C) 'Crest'. The view of the road is obscured by hedgerows.

128. You are driving along a country road where a 50 mph speed limit is in force. The traffic signs can be clearly seen, would you:

(A) Continue driving at the same speed?
(B) Use the mirrors and, if necessary, change position to just left of centre of the road when it is safe to do so, to gain a better view of the road ahead?
(C) Keep well to the left and should you meet any pedestrians or horses, sound the horn, continue driving at the same speed and expect them to move out of your way?

129. A concealed entrance warning sign can be seen on the right-hand verge. However, the entrance can actually be seen. Do you think the warning sign is:

(A) The correct distance from the potential danger?
(B) Too close to be of any use?
(C) On the correct side of the road?

130. A traffic sign can be seen. By looking well ahead, of what other advance information should you be aware? Using all available information how would you approach this situation?

(A) The time is shown on the clock tower, therefore look at your watch and compare the time.
(B) The sun is shining on the clock tower, with this in mind, you decide to wear your sunglasses.
(C) There is a steep downhill gradient ahead, therefore the mirrors should be used and speed reduced. A lower gear should be selected.

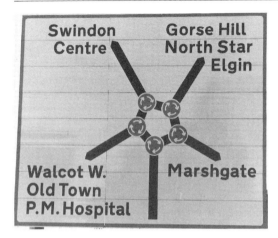

131. The traffic sign informs you that you are approaching a roundabout on a large gyratory complex. There is a two-way traffic system that circultes in a clockwise and anticlockwise direction. Who has the right of way at the mini-roundabouts?

(A) Traffic approaching from the right throughout the complex.
(B) Traffic approaching from the left.
(C) Traffic leaving Swindon Centre.

132. As you start to descend a steep hill, a traffic sign can be seen informing road users that there is an escape lane ahead. What is an escape lane, and what is its purpose?

(A) A special lane on the left to pull into, so that faster vehicles can overtake you.
(B) A place to stop, to view the countryside.
(C) A soft shoulder on the left that contains sand or shingle on to which you can steer, should the brakes fail.

133. This sign is situated on the pavement by the kerb. What is the purpose of the sign? Is it:

(A) To ask you to inform the police if you have seen something in your local newspaper regarding the accident?
(B) To tell you to contact the police station to find out what happened, if you are curious to know?
(C) To tell you to contact the local police station if you saw the accident or have any other information appertaining to it?

ROAD
MARKINGS

134. This section of a primary route has an additional lane for slow-moving vehicles. Who can use this lane?

(A) Heavy Goods Vehicles.
(B) Cyclists.
(C) Any vehicle.

135. The road has just been resurfaced, therefore no white lines or zebra crossing markings are present. In this situation is the zebra crossing a crossing or not?

(A) No it is not a zebra crossing.
(B) Not sure.
(C) Yes it is a zebra crossing.

136. The road ahead cannot be seen to be clear, therefore should you:

(A) Continue at the same speed and see what occurs?
(B) Look in the mirrors and reduce speed?
(C) Sound the horn as a warning of your presence?

137. This is a photograph of a dual carriageway that has a national speed limit of 70 mph. There is a long right-hand bend, at the apex of the bend a traffic sign has been demolished by a motor vehicle. The time of the accident was 11 pm, the road surface was wet. On the information given, how would you approach this bend?

(A) Select a lower gear on the bend, thereby using the gear as a brake.
(B) Continue driving at the same speed, and assume the tyres can cope with the road surface and speed.
(C) On seeing the bend, you should use the mirrors, look at the speedometer, and adjust your speed by deceleration or, if following traffic is present, use the brakes.

138. Slabs with grooves in them have been laid at the edge of the road. What are they called and what is their purpose?

(A) Water ducts: to allow rain water to quickly disperse from the road.
(B) Rumble strips: to warn road users of the potential danger of ill-defined verges.
(C) Anti-flooding slabs: to prevent water getting on to the road surface from the grass verge.

139. It has been raining, and wet leaves can be seen on the ground. What potential danger(s) arise in this situation?

(A) The road surface will be slippery and the kerb line ill-defined.
(B) Deep puddles cannot be seen.
(C) Shadows from the trees.

PEDESTRIANS

9

140. While driving along this country lane, you see pedestrians walking in the road. In this situation should you:

(A) Sound the horn and continue at the same speed?
(B) Make effective use of the mirrors and change course to pass them?
(C) Look in the mirrors, reduce speed, then sound the horn as a warning of your presence, and prepare to stop if required to do so.

141. The traffic signals at this pelican crossing are not working, so who has the right of way at the crossing – the drivers, or the pedestrians?

(A) None of them.
(B) The traffic.
(C) The pedestrians.

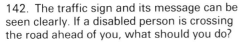

142. The traffic sign and its message can be seen clearly. If a disabled person is crossing the road ahead of you, what should you do?

(A) Continue driving at the same speed and sound the horn.
(B) Look in the mirrors and, should another vehicle be following, show your brake lights early with the intention of reducing speed and stopping if necessary.
(C) Look in the mirrors and give a signal of your intention to change course and pass the pedestrians, who could by now be in the middle of the road.

143. If pedestrians try to use this footpath, they will be confronted with overgrown hedgerows. This, combined with cones left by workmen, would make progress along the footpath potentially dangerous, particularly at night. As a pedestrian, how would you pass the cones?

(A) Wait on the footpath until the road is clear of traffic. Then pass the obstruction and return to the footpath.
(B) Walk into the road and expect drivers of approaching traffic to be aware of the obstruction on the footpath, and to allow a margin of safety as they pass you.
(C) Cross over to the other side of the road.

144. As you approach an infants' school, the school crossing patrol (lollipop lady) has her back to the road. A young child can be seen playing on the opposite side of the road, and on the wrong side of the guard rails. The mother of the child is seen talking to other people, and is not aware of the danger to the child. How should you approach this situation?

(A) Stop and tell the mother what you think of her.
(B) Continue driving at the same speed and sound the horn.
(C) Look in the mirrors, reduce speed and prepare to stop.

145. A pedestrian can be seen running across the road into the path of an approaching vehicle. Another pedestrian at the edge of the road is looking at the other pedestrian, and is not aware of your presence. Should you:

(A) Look in the mirrors, sound the horn and prepare to stop?
(B) Change course to steer round the pedestrian?
(C) Stop just before the pedestrian and invite him to cross the road?

146. As you approach a 'T' junction you can see refuse sacks on the road. A pedestrian and child are about to cross the road. Should you?

(A) Continue driving at the same speed and steer round the obstruction.
(B) Sound the horn and continue at the same speed.
(C) Look in the mirrors and reduce speed to make sure you can stop, when the pedestrians start to cross.

CYCLISTS

10

147. For what purpose has the continuous white line been laid?

(A) It marks a cycle path.
(B) To assist road users at night.
(C) It marks an additional footpath.

148. The car on the left is stopping to let an oncoming car through. A cyclist is passing and cuts in front of the car. Is the action taken by the cyclist correct?

(A) No, it is a dangerous manoeuvre.
(B) There is no need for the cyclist to wait.
(C) Yes.

149. Is the cyclist riding in the correct position on the road?

(A) Yes, for the prevailing conditions.
(B) No, he is too far from the kerb.
(C) No, he is too close to the hazard, in this case, a large puddle.

150. Is the cyclist in the correct position on the road?

(A) Yes.
(B) No.
(C) Not sure.

151. A cyclist can be seen trying to make progress on a very dangerous road surface. Should overtaking the cyclist be considered, and, if so, how would you anticipate making the manoeuvre?

(A) Give a long horn note to warn the cyclist of your presence.
(B) Look in the mirrors and accelerate to overtake as quickly as possible.
(C) If you must overtake, look in the mirrors and select a gear that will give maximum traction. Then adopt a position on the road that will give a good margin of safety.

152. Two cyclists can be seen ahead of you. What must you consider before deciding to overtake?

(A) The change in road surface.
(B) The 30 mph speed limits.
(C) What could appear round the bend ahead as you are about to overtake the cyclists.

153. The cyclist is carrying a long ladder. Is this legal or not?

(A) Legal, as it is the only way the ladder can be transported.
(B) Illegal, as the cyclist is not in full control of the cycle due to the load being carried.
(C) Not sure, as the cyclist may have an arrangement with the Police to use the cycle in the manner shown.

MOTOR CYCLISTS

155. As you negotiate a roundabout on a motorcycle, you see stones all over the road. What action should you take?

(A) Continue at the same speed.
(B) Brake hard to miss them.
(C) Look in the mirrors and, if safe to do so, reduce speed while keeping the machine upright, at the same time trying to avoid the hazard.

154. The young motorcyclist is receiving expert advice on machine maintenance. From the information in the photograph, what can the motorcyclist do to improve his *own* safety?

(A) Wear ankle length trainers.
(B) Wear sturdy trainers.
(C) Wear motorcycle boots.

157. The motorcyclist is going to pass a stationary car, and looks in the mirrors before a change of course is made. Is the rear observation being taken at the correct distance from the hazard?

(A) Yes.
(B) No, the motorcyclist is too close.
(C) Not sure.

156. There is no electric engine starter to this machine, the rider is therefore about to kick start the engine. What potentially dangerous fault is being committed while doing so?

(A) The rear wheel is off the ground.
(B) The rider is looking down.
(C) The centre stand is down.

158. This motorcyclist is going to turn right. What is the last thing the rider should do before changing course?

(A) Look over right shoulder (life-saver).
(B) Select a higher gear.
(C) Look in the mirror.

159. This novice motorcyclist is about to move off. What should he have done before getting on the motorcycle?

(A) Put on gloves.
(B) Put on motorcycle boots.
(C) Put on gloves, motorcycle boots and motorcycle jacket.

LEVEL
CROSSINGS

161. The driver is approaching an automatic open crossing without gates, barriers or attendant. No warning that a train is approaching has been given. Therefore how should this crossing be approached?

(A) Sound the horn and proceed over the crossing without reducing speed.
(B) Pull up at the stop line, then look and listen in both directions of the railway line. If clear move slowly forward, at the same time looking and listening.
(C) Continue driving as normal, as there is no danger of a train coming.

160. There is a level crossing ahead; no flashing warning lights can be seen. At what speed should you approach the crossing?

(A) The speed limit on this road is 50 mph, therefore it is safe to approach the crossing at the speed permitted by law.
(B) The road ahead is clear, therefore it is safe to continue driving at the same speed.
(C) Approach the level crossing at a moderate speed, so you can stop just before the barrier, should the need arise.

162. As this open level crossing is being approached, alternate flashing red lights can be seen. Is there any warning before the red lights start to flash?

(A) No.
(B) Yes, an amber flashing light.
(C) Yes, an audible warning followed by a flashing amber light.

163. As you approach a level crossing, flashing red lights can be seen and the barriers are lowered. What course of action should you take now?

(A) Make effective use of the mirrors and prepare to stop just after the wall.
(B) Select a lower gear and accelerate up to the barriers.
(C) Apply the brakes and stop.

164. This level crossing has no warning lights or barriers. A pedestrian has just passed through the gate, but has not closed it. Is the pedestrian in a hurry, considerate or thoughtless?

(A) In a hurry.
(B) Considerate.
(C) Thoughtless.

165. At this level crossing there are no special railway telephones or warning lights. Your intention is to drive over the crossing. What action should you take to do so safely, after stopping at the gate?

(A) Open the gates and sound the horn as you approach the crossing.
(B) Open the gates, and look and listen. If safe, proceed over the crossing, looking both ways as you do so.
(C) Open the gates and drive over the crossing. There is no need to check again, as it is obvious you are going over the crossing.

166. As you approach the level crossing, twin flashing red lights can be seen. Why are the red lights flashing? Is it because:

(A) A train is coming and the barriers are about to come down across the road? Therefore the mirrors should be used and you should prepare to stop.
(B) Flashing amber lights will be shown next, when they appear you may proceed across the crossing?
(C) The train has just passed, therefore you may accelerate away?

168. The driver has just overtaken a slower moving vehicle on the approach to a level crossing. How many offences have been committed? Is there any advice given in the *Highway Code* that relates to this situation?

(A) Two.
(B) Three.
(C) One.

167. As you approach the level crossing, flashing amber lights can be seen. Was any other warning given as the lights started to flash?

(A) An audible alarm.
(B) Flashing red lights.
(C) None.

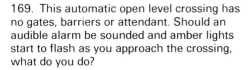

169. This automatic open level crossing has no gates, barriers or attendant. Should an audible alarm be sounded and amber lights start to flash as you approach the crossing, what do you do?

(A) Stop well before reaching the flashing lights.
(B) Select a lower gear and accelerate as quickly as possible.
(C) Stop in a position so that you can see what type of train is coming.

170. The driver of the vehicle has stopped to do some train spotting. Has the vehicle been parked in a safe place?

(A) No.
(B) Yes.
(C) Seems an ideal place to stop.

171. Alternately flashing red lights can be seen at this level crossing. How many other situations are controlled by alternate flashing red lights?

(A) Four.
(B) Six.
(C) Three.

172. The driver of this vehicle is deaf, and appears to have stalled the engine while on the crossing. For one reason or another he has decided to push the vehicle off the crossing. What should a driver do before pushing the vehicle off the crossing?

(A) Stop a passing motorist while on the crossing and explain the problem.
(B) Contact the signalman and explain what has happened and ask his advice on what could have stalled the engine.
(C) Contact the signalman and tell him the situation, and then try to remove the vehicle from the crossing.

173. The sign on the left can be seen clearly. But what colour are the lights that the sign refers to?

(A) White then amber.
(B) Amber then red.
(C) Green then blue.

STOPPING AND PARKING

13

174. The driver of this milk float made a mistake when he left the vehicle to make a delivery, and the float has finished up in this position. What do you think the mistake was?

(A) Hazard lights were not used.
(B) The vehicle was parked on a hill.
(C) The handbrake was not applied.

175. This vehicle is parked while the driver visits a friend. Is an offence being committed?

(A) No.
(B) Not sure.
(C) Yes.

176. The owner of this vehicle lives in a house near a junction. As there is nowhere else to park the car, the vehicle is parked on the road. Is the owner complying with the *Highway Code*?

(A) No.
(B) Not sure.
(C) Yes.

177. The driver of this vehicle has double parked in a one-way street to do some shopping. Hazard warning lights are being used to warn other road users of the obstruction. Are the hazard warning lights being used for the correct purpose?

(A) Yes.
(B) No.
(C) It is within the law to use hazard warning lights while parked.

178. A vehicle is being reversed on to a main road from a free standing place. What advice is given in the *Highway Code* regarding reversing on to a main road?

(A) You may reverse on to a main road provided it is safe to do so.
(B) It is inconsiderate to reverse on to a main road.
(C) Never reverse on to a main road, as it is potentially dangerous.

179. A car is parked at a junction. A vehicle should not be parked within a specified distance from a junction. What is the distance?

(A) 5 metres.
(B) 15 metres.
(C) 20 metres.

180. This vehicle is parked in a bus lane, it is not being loaded or unloaded. The time is 8 am on a Tuesday. Is an offence being committed?

(A) The vehicle has to be parked somewhere.
(B) No.
(C) Yes.

181. The motorcycle has been parked. Has it been parked correctly?

(A) Yes.
(B) The machine should have been turned round, with the front wheel nearest the kerb.
(C) No.

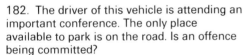

182. The driver of this vehicle is attending an important conference. The only place available to park is on the road. Is an offence being committed?

(A) No, the company who own the conference centre also own the piece of public road where the vehicle is parked.
(B) No, the driver has special permission from the boss.
(C) Yes, it is an offence to park at, or near a corner.

183. Numerous vehicles have been parked in a slip lane. Do you think the vehicles are legally parked?

(A) Yes, it seems a convenient place to park.
(B) No. The parked vehicles are causing an obstruction, obscuring other road users' views of the road to be joined.
(C) Not quite sure, take a chance and park in the slip lane, as there is adequate room for other road users to pass.

184. The driver of this vehicle has parked outside a private house. How many traffice offences are being committed?

(A) None.
(B) Four.
(C) Three.

185. The driver of the parked vehicle is waiting for his passenger to come back from the shops. Are any traffic offences committed in this situation? If so, how many?

(A) Two.
(B) Three.
(C) None.

186. There are yellow lines on the edge of the carriageway on both sides of the road, therefore, the van has been parked in the middle of the road on an area of white diagonal stripes. Has the van been parked legally?

(A) Yes.
(B) No.
(C) Yes, providing the driver has permission to do so.

187. The driver of this vehicle took a chance and is now going to pay for it. What offence has been committed?

(A) Unnecessary obstruction.
(B) Wilful obstruction.
(C) Parking on a yellow line.

BREAKDOWNS

14

188. Should a vehicle being driven develop an electrical fault and have to stop, the hazard warning lights cannot be used. The driver has placed a red reflecting triangle warning sign on the road. At what distance should the warning sign be placed from the vehicle?

(A) 10 metres.
(B) 20 metres.
(C) 50 metres.

189. If your vehicle were to break down just after a bend, should you place a triangle warning sign from the vehicle at the distance as suggested in the *Highway Code* or at a greater distance?

(A) As suggested in the *Highway Code*.
(B) At a greater distance.
(C) Nearer the vehicle.

TYRES

15

191. What is the legal minimum depth of a tyre tread and to what extent must the minimum tread cover the width and circumference of a tyre?

(A) 1 mm, covering 100% of the tread surface in contact with the road.
(B) 1 mm, covering 75% of the tread surface in contact with the road.
(C) 2 mm, covering 100% of the tread surface in contact with the road.

190. How often should tyre pressure and the condition of the tyres be checked?

(A) Every day.
(B) Once a week.
(C) Once a month.

192. The driver has brought the vehicle to rest with the front nearside tyre lodged against the kerb. In doing so could any damage be caused to the tyre?

(A) No.
(B) Yes. The inner casing that cannot be seen could be severely damaged, and thus induce a blow out at any time.
(C) No. Tyres are made to withstand this type of treatment.

ANIMALS

16

193. As you arrive at the stop line, your intention is to follow the road ahead, but cattle are being herded in front of you. What should you do?

(A) Move forward and at the same time rev the engine.
(B) Sound the horn and move forward.
(C) Wait on the stop line until the cattle are well clear of the junction, then move forward.

194. The horse and rider are on the pavement. Is this the correct place to ride a horse?

(A) Yes.
(B) No.
(C) Yes, providing pedestrians on the pavement move out of the way.

195. As you approach a horse and rider, you decide to overtake. What should you do to achieve your objective safely?

(A) Sound the horn and overtake with a gap of one and a quarter metres between your vehicle and horse and rider.
(B) Accelerate as hard as possible, in case the horse moves into your path.
(C) Look in the mirrors and, when safe to do so, move out allowing them plenty of room, and at the same time avoid revving the engine.

196. Your intention is to overtake the horse and rider. Do you consider it safe to do so, bearing in mind what can and cannot be seen? What would you do?

(A) Sound the horn and accelerate as quickly as possible.
(B) Sound the horn and expect the horse and rider to move to their left, allowing you more room to pass.
(C) Be patient and follow the horse and rider until the road ahead can be seen to be clear.

THE VEHICLE

17

197. It is the responsibility of the driver to ensure certain parts of a vehicle are kept clean. Which are they?

(A) The mirrors.
(B) The engine.
(C) The number plates, and all glass and lenses.

198. When do you think the fluid levels under the bonnet should be checked?

(A) Every day.
(B) Each week.
(C) Once a month.

199. The driver of this vehicle is loading numerous pieces of furniture on to the roof of an estate car. This load is obviously dangerous. Can it legally be transported?

(A) Yes, as the driver has no other means of transporting the furniture.
(B) No, the vehicle is not designed to carry this type of load. Also the load is insecure and, therefore, dangerous.
(C) Yes, provided the driver has control of the vehicle.

200. This vehicle is being driven on the public highway. Apart from the load on the roof is there an offence being committed?

(A) None.
(B) Two.
(C) Three.

201. This skip has been loaded with broken concrete. The contractor who filled the skip is waiting for it to be taken away. Is the skip load legal or not?

(A) Legal, the contractor is getting value for money.
(B) Legal, the weight of the load in the skip does not exceed that permitted by law.
(C) Illegal, the skip is overloaded, and therefore dangerous to other road users while being transported.

202. If 'L' plates have been fitted, should they be covered or removed when the vehicle is not being used for driving instruction or practice?

(A) No.
(B) Yes.
(C) Not sure.

203. The sign gives a warning to drivers of Heavy Goods Vehicles. What is it?

(A) Undulating road ahead.
(B) Uneven road.
(C) Sharp bend ahead.

204. You have got into the car and started the engine. What final check should you make before you move off?

(A) That the ignition warning light has gone off.
(B) That you have adequate fuel, and that the ignition and oil warning lights have gone off.
(C) That the oil warning light has gone off.

ANSWERS

18

1. C.
2. A.
   An alert driver travelling at 60 mph in a car that has good brakes, will need at least 240 feet to stop on a good dry road.
3. B.
4. B.
   Speed at the wrong time and in the wrong place was the prime factor that caused the accident.
5. A.
   It is of the utmost importance that a driver is aware of the presence and position of any following traffic at all times. Many serious and fatal accidents have occurred because of misuse of mirrors.
6. C.
7. C.
   There is a moped rider, who has not been seen, emerging from behind the nearside roof support pillar.
8. C.
   It is not advisable to punch a hole in the screen to improve vision, because this may cause injuries and aggravate the situation by allowing pieces of glass to enter the car. It must be borne in mind that the road ahead can still be seen when the windscreen shatters, so there is no need to panic. A laminated windscreen is safer than a toughened screen, because it is less likely to shatter.
9. A.
10. C.
    It is illegal and dangerous to exceed a weight limit as shown.

11. B.
    It must be borne in mind that your section of road is narrowed and another long vehicle could be following the one seen above. Therefore, use your mirrors, reduce speed and prepare to stop.
12. C.
13. A.
    Make effective use of your mirrors and reduce speed so that you can stop in the distance that can be seen to be clear.
14. C.
    A traffic sign can be seen that gives warning of two-way traffic. The road ahead cannot be seen to be clear, therefore it is not a safe place to overtake.
15. B.
16. B.
17. A.
18. C.
    The use of rear fog lamps should be used when visibility is less than 100 metres.
19. C.
    The driver should not overtake at a potentially dangerous place. In this case there is a junction on the right.
20. C.
21. B.
    It should be borne in mind there is a vehicle approaching, therefore the decision to overtake should not be made until the road ahead is clear. Overtaking should not take place within the confines of the zigzag area of the zebra crossing.

22. A.
    If both parties involved had taken an advanced riding/driving course, they would have been in the right place on the road, travelling at the right speed with the right gear engaged. They would be concentrating, planning ahead and riding/driving systematically, thus omitting no detail and leaving nothing to chance. If the system of car/motorcycle control had been complied with, the accident would never have occurred.
23. B.
    The circumstances are:
    1. When moving in or out of premises
    2. When moving in or out of a side road
    3. When ordered to do so by the police
    4. When ordered to do so by a traffic warden
    5. To avoid a stationary vehicle.
24. B.
    The driver has complied with the *Highway Code*. However, it is not good driving practice to proceed before the pedestrian has reached the pavement because a dangerous situation could occur.
25. C.
26. C.
    Due to concentrating on lighting the cigarette and not on driving the car, the driver could lose control of the vehicle.
27. B.
28. A.
    It is dangerous to overtake at, or near a junction.
29. B.
30. A.

31. C.
The pedestrian should give the driver plenty of time to see him/her, to slow down and to stop, before starting to cross the road.

32. A.

33. B.
The driver on the left is approaching a hazard and therefore should give the approaching driver right of way.

34. C.

35. C.
When the pedestrian came into view, the driver on the left should have used the mirrors and signalled his intention to change course to pass the pedestrian. This was not done. Because there was no driving plan the driver on the right thought it was safe to overtake, and in doing so created more danger.

36. C.
The driver has no consideration for any-one. Should a blow out occur on one of the tyres, especially the front, a serious or fatal accident could be the result, due to the casual manner in which the vehicle is being driven.

37. B.
38. A.
39. A.
40. A.
41. C.
42. B.
43. C.
44. C.
45. A.
46. A.
47. C.

48. C.
49. B.
50. A.
51. A.
52. B.
You should not invite a pedestrian to cross the road, as there could be other dangers present.

53. B.
54. C.
55. B.
It should never be assumed that a vehicle approaching from the right, signalling with its left-hand direction indicator, will actually turn left. You should wait for a reduction in speed or until the vehicle starts to turn, before deciding to move forward.

56. B.
Should a young child run out from between the vehicles, a car door open or a vehicle move away from the kerb, a serious accident could occur.

57. C.
Drivers must give way to pedestrians who are on the pavement.

58. B.
59. C.
60. C.
It is illegal and dangerous to reverse on a motorway or slip road, for any reason.

61. C.
Vehicles in the acceleration lane should give way to traffic on the motorway.

62. A.
63. B.
The two offences are:
1. The pedestrian should not be walking/running on the hard shoulder.
2. The motorist is being considerate but it is an offence to stop on a motorway except in an emergency.

64. C.
65. A.
66. B.
67. A.
68. C.
69. B.
The minimum stopping distance needed to stop from 50 mph is 175 feet. Here, therefore, no margin of safety has been allowed by the HGV drivers. Alternatively, an interval of two seconds should be left between vehicles travelling at a constant speed. This is known as the 'two-second rule'.

70. C.
71. C.
Heavy Goods Vehicles are prohibited to use the outside lane. Therefore the HGV in the outside lane is breaking the law.

72. B.
73. A.
It is an offence to use the hard shoulder at any time other than in an emergency or if directed to do so.

74. C.
75. C.
A gap of at least one metre for each mph must be maintained between the two vehicles, thus 40 mph = 40 metres. On wet roads the gap should be at least doubled.

76. C.
    The four dangers are:
    1. Hazard warning lights are not being used.
    2. Vehicles have been stopped too close to the carriageway.
    3. Pedestrians are standing/talking on the hard shoulder.
    4. A pedestrian can be seen directing traffic from the hard shoulder.
77. A.
78. C.
    1. Vehicles in the outside lane are following each other too closely, therefore allowing no margin of safety.
    2. No vehicles are using the middle lane. The outside lane should be used only for overtaking.
79. C.
    The mirrors should be checked and, if it is safe to do so reduce speed. In doing so, drop back from the vehicle in front, this will assist you to get clear of the spray and give you a better view of the road ahead.
80. A.
81. B.
82. A.
83. B.
84. C.
85. C.
86. B.
87. B.
88. A.
89. B.
90. B.
91. C.
92. A.

93. B.
    More than a door width is being allowed.
94. B.
    It is an offence to overtake the leading vehicle in the area marked by zigzag lines on the approach to a zebra crossing.
95. A.
    The road surface will be very slippery.
96. C.
97. C.
98. C.
99. C.
    By dropping back you will be in a position to see either side of the van, at the same time you will not be caught out should the van have to stop.
100. A.
    Common sense and good roadcraft must prevail when driving on this and any other road, regardless of whether road markings are present or not.
101. C.
102. A.
    The mirrors should be used and speed reduced, and a change of course made to the nearside.
103. C.
104. B.
    The driver has pulled into a passing place, allowing the approaching vehicle to pass. Common sense must prevail in all aspects of driving.
105. C.
106. B.
107. C.
108. C.
109. C.

110. C.
111. A.
112. C.
113. B.
114. B.
    The sign should not be ignored, as a fair warning has been given. Comply with the law.
115. B.
116. C.
117. A.
    The parents have parked too close to the school, opposite chevrons on the road and the car door is obstructing the footpath.
118. B.
119. C.
120. A.
121. C.
122. C.
    You are legally required to comply with a STOP sign.
123. B.
124. B.
125. C.
126. C.
127. B.
128. B.
129. B.
130. C.
131. A.
132. C.
133. C.
134. C.
135. A.
    It is a place to cross the road, but not a zebra crossing.
136. B.
137. C.

138. B.
139. A.
140. C.
141. C.
    The pedestrians have right of way when they are on the crossing, as it is now uncontrolled.
142. B.
143. A.
144. C.
145. A.
146. C.
147. A.
148. A.
    Should the car move off without the driver checking it is safe to do so, an accident will occur.
149. A.
    Common sense must prevail in certain conditions. You should ride past a deep puddle, not through it!
150. B.
    The cyclist should be using the cycle lane on the left.
151. C.
152. C.
153. B.
154. C.
155. C.
156. C.
    When pushing the machine off the stand, a sudden jolt could cause a gear to engage, allowing the machine to move off unexpectedly.
157. B.
    Effective observation must be taken at the right time and distance from the hazard; thereby allowing the rider time to react to changing circumstances.

158. A.
    A mirror has blind spots. Looking in the mirror will not show the motorcyclist the exact position of following traffic – looking over the shoulder will.
159. C.
    If the correct motorcycle clothing is not worn serious injury could result in the event of the rider coming off his machine.
160. C.
161. B.
162. C.
163. A.
164. C.
    Think of the dangers that can arise due to the gate being left open. A child or animal could wander on to the railway line in front of a train, the result inevitably would be fatal.
165. B.
166. A.
167. A.
    An audible alarm and flashing amber lights followed by a flashing red 'stop' sign, warn you when the barriers are about to come down.
168. B.
    The three offences are:
    1. Do not overtake at a level crossing.
    2. Approach a level crossing at a moderate speed.
    3. The road ahead cannot be seen to be clear.
169. A.
170. A.
    A vehicle should not be stopped immediately beyond any level crossing.
171. B.

1. Level crossings. 4. Fire stations.
2. Lifting bridges. 5. Motorways.
3. Airfields.   6. Cattle crossings.
172. C.
    It must be borne in mind that the driver is deaf. After the vehicle has been removed from the crossing, the signalman must somehow be informed that the crossing is clear.
173. B.
174. C.
175. C.
    It is an offence to park a vehicle on any section of road marked with double white lines even if one of the lines is broken.
176. A.
    It is illegal to park at or near a junction.
177. B.
    Hazard warning lights must not be used or regarded as providing an excuse for stopping when you should not.
178. C.
179. B.
180. C.
    It is an offence to park a vehicle in a bus lane during the times and days shown on the sign, except to load or unload goods when permitted.
181. C.
    The motorcycle should be parked with wheels parallel to the kerb.
182. C.
183. B.
184. C.
    A driver should not park at, or near, a school entrance, on a brow of a hill or where areas of white diagonal stripes have been painted on the road.

185. A.
1. It is an offence to park a vehicle within the area marked by zigzag lines on either side of a zebra crossing.
2. The cyclist should have stopped for the pedestrians on the crossing.
186. B.
187. C.
188. C.
189. B.
190. A.

It is important that tyre pressure and the condition of the tyres are checked daily, despite the fact that modern tyres retain their pressure for long periods. It is a legal requirement that pressure is correctly maintained at all times, and is especially important before any long journey is undertaken.

191. A.
192. B.
193. C.

Patience and common sense must prevail. When the cattle are clear of the junction you can move forward, providing it is safe to do so.

194. B.
195. C.
196. C.
197. C.
198. A.

Especially when contemplating an arduous journey.

199. B.
200. B.
1. The load inside the vehicle is insecure, and could fall on to the road.
2. The rear number plate cannot be seen, as required by the law.
201. C.
202. B.
203. C.

The sign warns drivers of HGVs that there is a sharp bend ahead, therefore speed should be reduced to minimise the possibility of overturning the vehicle.

204. B.

How many did you get right?

If you answered less than 100–110 correctly then you pose a considerable threat to road safety and should take remedial action immediately. You should seek advice on and assistance in improving your driving skills. The Institute of Advanced Motorists and RoSPA Advanced Drivers Association have voluntary groups all around the country and would be pleased to offer advice or enrolment details for their many driving courses.

If you answered between 110 and 170 then you would be advised to brush up on the *Highway Code*. This will make you a safer and more courteous driver.

If you scored between 170 and 204 you deserve a pat on the back – well done! You should survive and help others to survive on the roads.

Further titles written by the author include: *Advanced Driving*; *Pass The Driving Test*; and *Take Your Car Abroad*.

Institute of Advanced Motorists
IAM House
359/365 Chiswick High Road
London W4 4HS
Tel: 01-994 4403

RoSPA Advanced Drivers Association
Cannon House
The Priory
Queensway
Birmingham B4 6BS
Tel: 021-200 2461